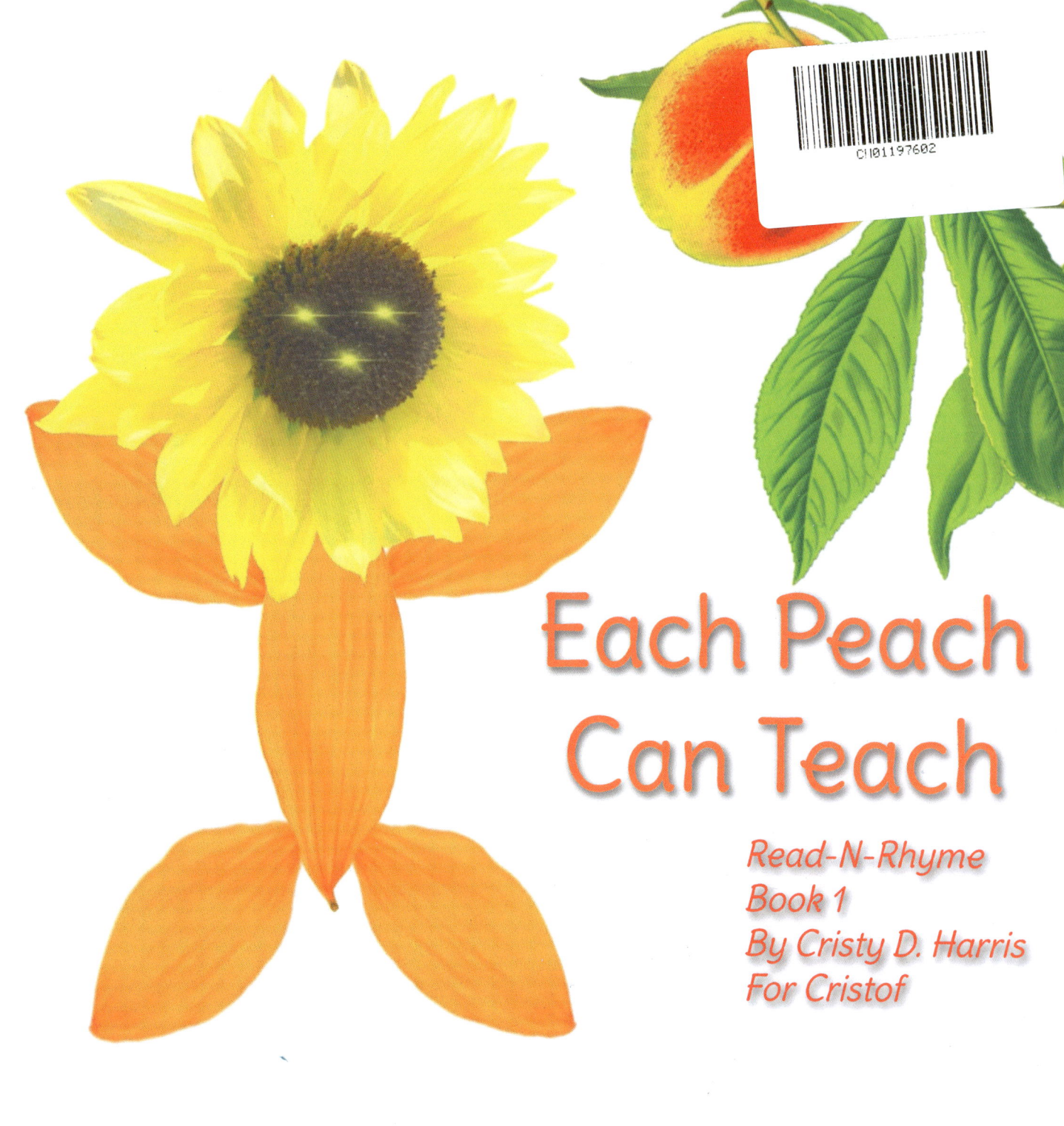

Each Peach Can Teach

Read-N-Rhyme
Book 1
By Cristy D. Harris
For Cristof

Can you
pick the
peach?

Now plop it on the "p" in...

Peach.

Without the "p" each peach would simply not be.

Let's reach for the peach.

And take it to the beach.

If you push your peach into the beach...

the
peach
juices
may
leach...

leaving behind a sticky beach.

What
fun
things
each
peach
on a
beach
can
teach.

Each

Peach

Teach

Reach

Beach

Leach

Printed in Great Britain
by Amazon

53375888R00016